Free Verse Editions

Edited by Jon Thompson

MAN PRAYING

Poems

Donald Platt

Parlor Press
Anderson, South Carolina
www.parlorpress.com

Parlor Press LLC, Anderson, South Carolina, 29621

Library of Congress Cataloging-in-Publication Data

Names: Platt, Donald, 1957- author.
Title: Man praying : poems / Donald Platt.
Description: Anderson, South Carolina : Parlor Press, [2017] | Series: Free
  verse editions | Includes bibliographical references.
Identifiers: LCCN 2017038742 (print) | LCCN 2017038931 (ebook) | ISBN
  9781602358829 (pdf) | ISBN 9781602358836 (epub) | ISBN 9781602358843 (
  ibook) | ISBN 9781602358850 (mobi) | ISBN 9781602358812 (pbk. : acid-free
  paper)
Classification: LCC PS3566.L286 (ebook) | LCC PS3566.L286 A6 2017 (print) |
  DDC 811/.54--dc23
LC record available at https://lccn.loc.gov/2017038742

978-1-60235-881-2 (paperback)
978-1-60235-882-9 (pdf)
978-1-60235-883-6 (epub)

2 3 4 5

Cover design by David Blakesley.
Cover image: Chaim Soutine, *L'Homme en prière*. (The Man in Prayer). 1921-1922. Oil on canvas. 51 x 25 1/2 in.
  (129.5 x 64.8 cm). Portrait of M. Racine., oil on canvas, Private Collection. © 2017 Estate of Chaim Soutine /
  Artists Rights Society (ARS), New York."
Printed on acid-free paper.

Parlor Press, LLC is an independent publisher of scholarly and trade titles in print and multimedia formats. This book
is available in paperback and ebook formats from Parlor Press on the World Wide Web at http://www.parlorpress.
com or through online and brick-and-mortar bookstores. For submission information or to find out about Parlor
Press publications, write to Parlor Press, 3015 Brackenberry Drive, Anderson, South Carolina, 29621, or email
editor@parlorpress.com.

Contents

for Dana, Eleanor, and Lucy

Acknowledgments

My thanks to the editors of the following publications in which these poems, sometimes in slightly different versions, first appeared:

BLOOM: "Like Jacob at Peniel"

Crazyhorse: "Lighthouse Digest Doomsday List"

Ecotone: "Eurydice in Hell"

Green Mountains Review: "Christ's Entry into Brussels in 1889," "One Page Torn from the Book of the Names of the Dead" (each featured as a "poem of the week" on the journal's website)

Gulf Coast: "Caravaggio's *Beheading of St. John the Baptist*"

Passages North: "Offering Red"

Prairie Schooner: "23 Quai de Voltaire," "Every Touch"

Seneca Review: "Die Krüppelmappe," "La Playa los Muertos"

Shenandoah: "The *Davydov*"

Southwest Review: "The Main Event"

Sou'wester: "Aubade with Foley Catheter"

VOLT: "Playing Badminton with Eleanor"

Western Humanities Review: "Frozen Assets," "Fugitive Pigment"

"The Main Event" was reprinted in *The Best American Poetry 2015* (Scribner).

I am grateful to the National Endowment for the Arts for an individual artist's fellowship and to Purdue University for an Artistic Endeavors Fellowship, both of which greatly aided in the completion of this book. Thanks to Mary Leader for offering spot-on advice about some of these poems and to Dana Roeser for her crucial input on many of the poems and on the book as a whole. I am indebted to my family—Eleanor and Lucy Platt and Dana Roeser—for their love and support.

MAN PRAYING

Eurydice in Hell

                    I like to think
Eurydice when she walked up the long, steep, stony path
                    out of hell

only a few feet behind Orpheus—weak man who could not help
                    but turn—
and saw the dim light brighten all around her

                    into dawn,
and heard the first fat robin's chortle, and smelled the blooming
                    overworld, pear trees

white as a snowstorm's freeze frame . . . I like to think Eurydice
                    walked on sharp
stones and gravel strewn with petals fallen from star

                    magnolias that bent
their high heavens over her. I would spare her bare feet from hurt
                    with those petals'

royal rags, ripped silk—white on one side, veined with pink lavender
                    on the other.
In the same way, I want to protect Eleanor, our bipolar

                    daughter, who is recovering
from a manic break last November. Her meds doc has weaned her
                    off of Seroquel,

antipsychotic. She's taking 600 mg of lithium twice a day,
                    this therapeutic dose
close to toxic. She has her blood drawn every four weeks

to check her lithium
level. She hovers at point 9. She too has been walking the stone path barefoot
out of hell. No white

and lavender-pink petals, starting to turn brown at their edges,
will stop her feet
from getting cut and bleeding. If it would do any good,

I would go down
on my knees and bathe those white, bruised feet—both Eleanor's
and Eurydice's—

wash off with water from hell's hot springs the crusted blood,
mud, the caked
volcanic ash. I would clean the black pustulant bite on her right heel

from the asp
that sent her down to hell on her wedding night. As she escalated
into mania,

she called Orpheus long-distance, her French boyfriend in Provence,
to yell and cry
at how he was neglecting her, couldn't "commit" to their

relationship.
Now that she's descended to the underworld, he wants to "save"
her, has bought her

a plane ticket to France, against her doctors' advice, for a three-month
visit. They say
she has to get her blood checked, needs more therapy. It takes two years

for the brain to recover
from a manic episode with psychotic features. It's May. I've changed
          her return-trip flight

so she stays five weeks. Orpheus can't support her, works in a meat-packing
          plant, lives with his parents,
gets stoned every day. Pot is a trigger for her mania.

          Of course, Orpheus—
that narcissist—will look back to make sure that she is following him.
          Eurydice will cry out, wave,

and disappear into the shadows. Orpheus will go get stoned
          again. The path
back to hell is switchback. Her bare feet will trample

          the star magnolias'
petals until they turn to a brown pulpy mess. Neither Orpheus
          nor I can bring her

back. Eleanor needs her own God-given myth. Would that my footsore
          beggar poem
might sing her up from the ground with the redbud. May

          she rise every April
from the dark kingdom, hypomanic as spring, like azaleas shouting
          and shedding

red words so that the green leaves come. Or I will
          go down to stay
with her, my grievous daughter, where roots sleep winter out.

Every Touch

Out of the dirt
red roses grow and reach their brambly rambling arms
up and around

the downspout and trellis on the west side of our front porch.
They make a scrim
of green serrated leaves and red velvet blossoms, a tapestry

of shade, light,
and perfume when the wind blows right on this May morning.
I sit on the blue

wood-slat swing, suspended by chains from the porch's ceiling,
and waste another
hour. Nothing better to do, I count 189 roses, lose track,

start again. I think
of conceptual artist Jim Hodge's "flower curtains." He bought silk flowers,
peeled the petals

and leaves from their wire and plastic stems, ironed them flat.
His assistants
at the Fabric Workshop and Museum in Philadelphia

glued paper towels
to form a sheet, fourteen by sixteen feet. To it Hodges pinned
his silk petals and leaves

like butterfly specimens. Where their edges touched, the assistants
sewed them together
with bar tack stitches on sewing machines. Then they pulled away

the paper-towel backing
and were left with lacework of silk pansies, violets, tulips,
                    peonies, geraniums, poppies,

chrysanthemums, zinnias, daisies, roses, day lilies, all
                    interspersed with green leaves.
Every Touch, Hodges called it. He said, "I felt that if the flowers

                    were deconstructed . . . flattened
out and brought back to 'fabricness,' they would suggest a cycle—
                    a life cycle . . . that maintained

or maintains every touch of its existence." The curators say
                    he was thinking
of his assistants' fingers gently guiding the petals under

                    the piston-like needles
of their sewing machines and—go further—of workers' hands
                    cutting blossoms from bolts

of dyed silk in some sweatshop. No, I say it was his lover's
                    hand unbuttoning
his shirt, touching his nipples until they hardened to the stems

                    of honeysuckle taken
between teeth. So that his lover might sip nectar there.
                    It was all his other

lovers and their lovers stitched to one another
                    by touch,
each one a blue iris, calla lily, or bird of paradise

          unrivaled in the unraveling
skein of years. The nectar went viral. Felix Gonzalez-Torres,
            artist who had helped

to get Jim the residency at the Fabric Workshop and Museum,
            finally died
from "AIDS complications" in 1996. Famously, Felix

           had heaped up
175 lbs. of hard candy, his dead lover Ross Laycock's "ideal weight,"
            in a gallery's corner

and let each viewer pick a brightly-wrapped piece and eat it, partake
            of Ross's sweet flesh,
ingest his death and be complicit in it, the pile

           decreasing
just as Ross's body had wasted away. He'd found the unforgettable
            metaphor for what

AIDS did—guilt slash ecstasy slash grief. On twenty-four billboards
            throughout New York City
he put a blown-up black-and-white photo of an unmade

           queen-size bed
with two pillows. The rumpled sheets and dented pillows seemed
            to hold and darkly halo

the two invisible bodies. He merged public and private. When asked,
            "Who is your public?"
Felix replied, "I say honestly, without skipping a beat, 'Ross.'"

When asked, "So are you
in love now?" Felix shot back, "I never stopped loving Ross.
                    Just because he's dead

doesn't mean I stopped loving him. . . . Every lesion he got
                    I loved him more."
The day Felix died, almost five years after Ross, Jim Hodges

                    drew flowers
 in black, red, and blue ink on twenty-four paper napkins of different sizes
                    and pinned them

to a white wall. His final flower curtain was all black.
                    He called it *The end
from where you are*. Look closely. You'll see a few yellow

                    and blue petals showing
through the black. The living stitch themselves to the dying.
                    Felix told Ross,

"I want to be there until your last breath." Ross asked him
                    for pills to commit
suicide. Felix wouldn't give the pills to him and said, "Honey,

                    you have fought hard
enough. You can go now. You can leave. Die." They were at home.
                    "I was there to his last breath."

Touch the black flower curtain, and a tremor will rip,
                    ripple the fabric.
Through it, see the people on the other side look back at you.

Offering Red

Mary Hambleton, 1952-2009

I am a red box, fifteen by four by two inches, with six bright blue stripes painted lengthwise

*

I contain nothing

*

Along one of my edges runs a long three-dimensional seam of black oil paint spattered with
    yellow, green, blue, red, gray, and olive: dried lava

*

It is as if the lava has oozed through a crack in the box

*

Someone has passed a paintbrush, holding only a few traces of black paint, over my blue
    stripes so that each bristle leaves its own distinct swirl

*

Black switchbacks

*

The blue stripes are my staves

*

The black brushstrokes make the only musical notation

*

Here is what I have to give you: twenty-two small red wooden blocks heaped haphazardly on
        my upward-facing side

*

One block has one blue face; another block has one black dot

*

The black dot is my offering

I am lost, I am not making the drawing, but the drawing is making itself and making me make it

Fifteen rectangles
arranged in three rows of five
        with PET scans—

Positron
Emission Tomography—
        of Mary Hambleton's

        body on each
rectangle and half-painted
        over with white so

she becomes
a naked woman seen through
cold mist, hot steam from

a shower.
Superimposed on all these
selves, target pattern

of gray and
white concentric circles. Dots—
black, white, or gray holes—

riddle each
woman. Here is melanoma's
shooting range, silence.

The upper-left-hand
rectangle has been painted
black with three

white dots. This woman
becomes someone's game of
dominoes.

I had a child. Suddenly there was intense color in my life and it gradually entered into my work. It's been progressively important to allow myself to do what comes into my head

She balanced children's blocks, which she had repainted and on which she sometimes glued
      images, along the tops of many of her paintings

                                        *

The blocks are always falling off the pictures

                                        *

The gallery guard has to pick them up. He arranges the blocks differently each time he puts
      them back

                                        *

In this way he becomes part of her painting

                                   Four pairs of
                        vertical and parallel
                              orange-yellow lines

                                   intersect
                        a blue field. Scribbled squiggles
                              of a darker blue

                                   suggest dusk,
                        abrupt swallows flying low,
                              swerving into and

out of a red barn's
black windows and doors without
one wasted

wingbeat. Moon, thumbprint
cut through by orange-yellow
lines, rises.

On top of her 2007 painting *Target*, Mary Hambleton sets four cubes of different sizes. One
is egg-yolk-yellow with a few flecks of red to fertilize it. Two are off-white

*

On top of the larger of these two, she scrapes dried, crusted, off-white paint from her palette
with a palette knife and leaves it there

*

On four sides of the last cube, she has pasted four identical digital photographs of an etching
of a dodo, with a non-extinct bird—possibly a robin—perched on a branch over the
dodo's head

*There is a root word, **Mirus**, which I have used to title a series of drawings. It comes from the Latin word for wonder*

In this dark
time-lapse photography—*I've*
been given a new

reality—four
scans stand, each in its own
panel. Read

right to left,
the figures grow more ghostly.
One that I keep

waiting to
go away, but it doesn't.
The last one becomes

a sine curve
of browned-out light. Below them,
stripes of primary

colors and
orange, green, white, gray, and plum
arranged like the keys

on a xylophone.
A child will pick up her mallet,
play blacker

melodies
upon these color-coded
keys. *It's now part of*

---

who I am.
Bend close to listen. White dots,
one red dot remain.

A circle is a circle, but it is also a moon, a planet, and the world

Two scans, white against their black negative, are surrounded by twelve squares, each
        containing the same colored print of the extinct ivory-billed woodpecker perched on
        one branch and pecking at another branch

*

I imagine I am Mary

*

The two limbs form a Y

*

I reverse every other print so that each ivory-billed woodpecker on the top and bottom rows
        looks toward another to form a pair bond

*

The woodpeckers can face only one way

*

Black dots like bullet holes through the prints. The hunter keeps missing. No, it is a shooting
      gallery

*

I retouch each woodpecker with random white splotches

*

Not ivory

*

The white paint drips in six long streaks over the negative, black bedroom from which the
      two scans stare out

*

But not at me

Sun lowers.
Alizarin red, drench me
before I am quenched.

Below two small scans, a row of squares within larger squares: red within light blue within
      red within black within beige

*

They vibrate

*

I am a passenger borne on a wind yet to come

*

Purple within royal blue within lavender within black within lavender, like Amish quilts.
    Each is big as a little finger's nail

*

I insert into the row of colored squares two white squares on which the same black-and-gray
    passenger pigeon is etched

*

Wind, neither northwest by north, nor southeast by east

*

It carries me toward no known point on the compass rose

White bubbles
from an unseen deep-sea diver's
respirator, swirls

of black current, gray
eels twisting on themselves like
the small

                          intestines'
             swollen coils. How to fathom
                    body? One gob of

                          spit is what
             the sun becomes from this far
                    down, darker star's shine.

Then there's a lot that I find horrific. We terrify me as human beings

One block painted a silvery lavender gray with the digital photograph, glued to one face, of a
        black-and-white hand holding a small, white, bird's egg

                                    *

The fingers are starting to curl up loosely around the egg, held on the flat of the palm, as if
        to protect it

                                    *

A large block painted white with the endangered African forest elephant depicted in black on
        one white face

                                    *

The image looks like scrimshaw on an ivory tusk

Bright box that
contains my whole day—French's
mustard-yellow on

one side, then
watermelon-pink picnic
on the opposite

side. Blue sky
on box's top and bottom.
For half an hour I

let the blue
top drip across the white front
so it looks as if

hard rain has
made a woman's long blue hair
fall, stream down her face.

The line was intentionally mercurial. It is just a line, it is just a stroke of paint, but it could be a figure, a female form

Along the top edge, five feet long, of her last painting, 2008, Mary Hambleton lines up
twenty-three blocks

MAN PRAYING

*

They reprise all the motifs of her last seven years

*

On a child's toy blocks she glues digital images of dodos, passenger pigeons, African forest
    elephants, ivory-billed woodpeckers, and the hand holding its egg

*There was this quietude. I was in the studio with the barn doors open, no music, just listening to the
sounds of the trees, of wind*

On the faces of the faint gray suns—two whole suns and two halves of suns—are black
    dots

*

Wormholes

*

In the June before she died, her vision clouded, "became severely impaired"

*

Within the circles and half-circles of her last suns are also white dots. Emily Dickinson's.
    "Soundless as dots—on a Disc of Snow—"

*

In October her vision cleared

*

The only spot of different color is the red crest of the ivory-billed woodpecker on its block

*

The white dots are nails driven into hard maple flooring, their heads then puttied over

The critic Bill Zimmer once said to me, "Small paintings are seen directly by the soul"

She died on January 9th in New York City. It was not snowing

*

In the line of twenty-three blocks, she put one white plaster sphere, two inches in diameter: dodo's egg

*

Symmetrical to the dodo's egg, Mary set a paper ball, the same size as the egg, two blocks in on the right side of the line of blocks. It is made of her discarded, white, painter's tape

*

No, it's not white

*

It is ivory

*

Unwind the tape, walk backward through the dark labyrinth until you come to the door you
    entered at birth

Enough unprimed sky

*

Enough nausea like morning sickness all day long

*

Enough sidewalk's off-white concrete splotched with the first fat Rorschach drops of rain

My black globs of oil
paint look like slag from a blast
furnace, which

you splattered
with gouts of greens, reds, ultra-
marines. Stuck into

the slag, three
dried seed pods—opened, emptied.
Bronzed petals. The seeds

you embedded in
my black dirt, eight brown BB
pellets, then

drove thirteen
rusted six-penny nails at
odd angles into

my wood box
so that they stick up, spikes you
must now walk barefoot.

Mary asked her doctor for a copy of her 169th scan. She wanted to surround it with colored
    dots

*

The ball of ivory tape casts its round gray shadow on the lighter gray of the gallery wall

*

Ken Buhler, Mary's husband, recalled how near the end "at one point she just looked up and
    said, *Dots will somehow always be important*"

                    Three, always
        three. Beauty, truth, etcetera.
                    One to spin the thin

                    black thread, another
        to measure it, and the last
                            to cut it

                        short. Wait here,
        watch. Three scans' silhouettes face right.
                    Azure circulates

                    through the first woman's
        spinal column. Blue serpent
                            coils around

                    her cold uterus.
        The second is black and white.
                            Cerebrum's

                    thunderhead will drop
        rain and hail, flatten the crops.
                            The third is

                    simple skeleton.
        Ave, Mary Hambleton,
                            pray for us.

I love how I can move from a small mark to the grand sweep, how varied the touch can be, how endless

---

As if butcher block
were hacked, scratched, carved with swirls like
fingerprints,

brandings, coins,
then the left side painted black,
the right side gold.

They are mirrors and windows and worlds to get lost and found in; I want to hold you as long as I can

Die Krüppelmappe

I.

A couple with foreheads pressed together, eyes
closed. The man has a scraggly goatee, bald head,

wrinkled brow. The woman's hair is pulled into
a bun. Two sticks hold it in place. Her earrings,

the shape of falling women, men, or angels,
hang from drooping earlobes. His down-turned mouth

says nothing. Her hands caress his amputated
left hand's prosthesis, steel hook mounted on a

leather cuff that laces like a calf-high boot
up to his elbow. Will she unlace and kiss

his prosthesis, then lick the pink stump, skin flaps
sewn together like the dough of an oozing

brown sugar-cinnamon roll whose ends have been
pinched shut? What foreplay, silences, pained

hesitations, tremors are theirs? Whose hand
can draw their love or map this crippling?

II.

One year after the Great War, Heinrich Hoerle
made twelve lithographs, black grease pencil on stone,

called them *The Cripple Portfolio*, and got
the city of Cologne to print it. He also

drew a naked man without arms, pegs for feet,
seated on a satin-backed Windsor chair. His

penis is tucked between his legs so we can't
see it. He gapes down at the floor, at six clay

flowerpots from which pairs of hands and feet grow.
The hands gesticulate, clench, open, beckon.

The feet kick. They flower into fingers, pink
toes. The man stares, starts to scream. He wakes up. He

still has no arms, no feet. The hands and feet still
strain from their clay flowerpots, stretch toward him.

III.

In another lithograph, another man—
naked, right leg amputated at the knee—

lies on his back on a settee, which has snakes
for its legs. His eyes are closed. His left arm curls

around his bald head, pillowed on the settee's
one armrest. With his right hand he holds his stump

so it points upward. He has no cock, only
the smooth mons veneris of a woman who

has shaved her pubic hair. His amputated
leg becomes a thick, gigantic hard-on, which

the man slowly strokes. It has the swollen shape
of a sleek bomb or missile, perhaps the one

to which the man lost half his leg. The cock or
stump comes to a point, and this tip is shaded

dark with the grease pencil. His stump ejaculates
straight up. The jet of come becomes an empty

tea cup and saucer. From the cup's center shoots
a tall stalk like a fountain. It bifurcates,

grows two leaves. Between them emerges a foot—
heel, ball, and bald big toe. It is that painful

moment of release, wordless yes, when the sperm
splatters over chest and abdomen. The man

whispers only, "Lost foot, clubfoot, come home!" No,
he groans someone's name, spasm after spasm.

IV.

Michael, my brother who has Down syndrome, sat
on the same orange-brown couch in our living

room for seventeen years. All day he'd listen
to long-playing records of Broadway show tunes.

His favorite was *Hello, Dolly*. He'd sway
to Carol Channing belting out, "It's so nice

to be back home where I belong!" Michael lived
with our parents for forty-three years until

my father's stroke. My aging mother could no
longer care for them. They went to a nursing

home and a halfway house. Where do we belong?
With whom? What night will finally house us? Who

will sing the chorus? "You're still glowin', you're still
crowin', you're still goin' strong. . . ." My brother goes

home to our mother's house for day visits. They
sit together on the old couch and listen

to *Hello, Dolly*. "You're looking swell, Manny."
I remember how once years ago Michael

rubbed his hard cock through his half-unzipped pants
while resting on the couch after a big lunch.

Mom and I sat in our rocking chairs and kept
talking. Dolly sang, "So bridge that gap, fellas.

Find me an empty lap, fellas." When Michael
reached orgasm, he threw his head back and panted

like a dog lapping water from a puddle
on a July day. As he masturbated,

did he imagine Mom or Carol Channing
naked? Did he have images at all? Or

did he keep his eyes open and, when he came,
see what's always there before us if we look?

Walls, table, chairs, ceiling, and through the picture
window a crab apple tree blooming. Mom said,

"Come, Michael. Let's go change your underwear and
trousers." Dolly'll never go away again.

V.

In Heinrich Hoerle's next-to-last lithograph
of *The Cripple Portfolio*, another

naked man masturbates his amputated
left leg. This stump too ejaculates straight up.

The sperm's jet becomes the roots of a green
sapling, whose five branches bear leaves and apples.

A woman in a dress so sheer we can see
her breasts, buttocks, and tufted pudendum, all

in profile, reaches both hands up for the ripe
apples. The ringlets around her forehead are

carefully drawn. She has a long aquiline
nose and eyes set slightly too close together.

Is she Heinrich's wife, Angelika, whom he
will abandon when she contracts TB? She

walks in high heels across the plowed ground. The man
lies prone on the new-turned field. The sapling springs

from his loins. She tastes the tart fruit. Her red mouth
waters. She gorges, always reaches for more.

The man is sinking back into the dirt, whose
furrows lap him like ocean waves, enwomb him.

Caravaggio's *Beheading of St. John the Baptist*

              Caravaggio too knew
that violence and murder underlie religion, eroticism, all
              civilization. See

how in this dark, poorly lit picture—the largest canvas he ever
              painted, which takes up
nearly the whole wall above the altar in the Oratory

              at St. John's Co-Cathedral
in Valletta—the executioner has botched the job. He's dropped
              the sword that wasn't sharp

enough to sever the spine and neck tendons completely
              and reaches behind
his back to pull out of the leather sheath that hangs

              from his belt
the dagger they call a *miserere*. "Have mercy upon me, O God,
              according to thy loving-kindness."

He lifts St. John's long hair in his left fist to clear the neck
              for one clean stroke
and hack through the last stubborn sinews. He's workmanlike—

              his forehead furrowed
with concentration, concerned with getting the job done right this time
              around. The jailor wears yellow

tights and a fancy ultramarine jacket over a brown tunic. Four
              large skeleton keys
dangle from his sash, phalli that won't fit into his ample

codpiece. He offers quiet
advice to the executioner and points with his right forefinger, caught
in the shaft of sunlight

penetrating the dim courtyard outside the jail's gate, to the gold platter
the young maid
holds. She's bending low to make it easier to hoist

the severed head
onto her serving tray and bear it, as ordered, to King Herod
and Salome.

Postprandial palate cleanser. To please her lustful stepfather
on his birthday, Salome
did a lap dance and got him to grant whatever she desired.

She said what her mother,
Herodias, told her to ask for—the prophet's head upon
a platter. Easy

as a pig in a blanket. Herod waved one hand, and it was done.
But in Caravaggio's
canvas, there remain these technical difficulties. The old woman

to the left of the jailor
clasps her head in both hands and closes her eyes at what occurs
next. She'd thought

that during her eighty-five years on earth she'd seen it all and couldn't be
surprised by anything
else. She's wrong. The painting is understatement and silence.

                        The artist's famous
light, his chiaroscuro, plays on the executioner's strong bare back,
                        ribs, and left shoulder,

the deltoid Caravaggio would have liked to kiss and run
                        his tongue along.
It also underlines the underside of the maid's

                        frail upper arm.
Beauty and terror converge, as always. Caravaggio would have heard
                        the stories of how

during the Great Seige of Malta, forty years before he painted
                        this beheading,
La Valette, Grand Master of the Order of the Knights of St. John,

                        for whom the new city
of Valletta would be named, had ordered the dead Turks
                        to be decapitated.

The knights then stuffed those heads into their cannons and shot
                        them back as cannon balls
against the Sultan's forces massed below the ramparts

                        of Fort St. Elmo.
The gunpowder-seared skulls would have been unrecognizable.
                        John the Baptist's face,

eye-level with the celebrant at the Oratory's altar,
                        is tranquil,
beautiful. His hands are still bound behind his back with a length

of rope that undulates
from under his legs like a snake slithering quickly away.
                    Evil is erotic and always

with us. Inveterate brawler, Caravaggio had killed
                    Ranuccio Tomassoni
in a duel in Rome. He fled to Malta, via Naples,

                    with a *bando capitale*
issued against him. If he had been apprehended, he would have been
                    beheaded. To keep

their heads intact in combat, the Knights of the Order of St. John
                    wore tempered-steel
helmets with cabled combs, plume holders, visors, upper and lower

                    bevors that swiveled
on pivot nuts, sight slits, riveted gorgets to protect
                    their necks,

and breath holes. They had their helmets engraved with acanthus leaves,
                    fleurs-de-lis, coronets,
coats of arms, rams locking horns. If they died, they died

                    in style. John the Baptist
didn't. He wore only a loincloth of mangy fur and a crimson
                    cloak that's slid

from his shoulders. The executioner's bare dirty left foot
                    stands on the cloak.
From a large barred window, two speechless prisoners watch

                    the executioner prepare
to finish the beheading. Caravaggio has signed the painting
                    with the prophet's

blood pooling below the half-severed head. He had only two years left
                    to live. He wrote
his name in the blood of men he loved, murdered, and would have died for.

The Main Event

At the weigh-in
on the morning of March 24th, 1962, the World Welterweight Champ,
Benny "Kid" Paret,

called his challenger, Emile Griffith, a *maricón* –
Cuban slang for "faggot"—
and smiled. Emile wanted to knock the Kid out right there.

Gil Clancy, his manager,
managed to hold him back, told him to "save it for tonight."
The New York Times

wouldn't print the correct translation, maintained that Paret had called
Emile an "unman."
The sportswriter Howard Tuckner raved against the euphemistic

copy editors, "A butterfly
is an unman. A rock is an unman. These lunatics!"
No one would mention

the word "homosexual" in connection with a star
athlete. Another
journalist, Jimmy Breslin—Irish straight-talker—said,

"That was what Paret
was looking to do—get him steamed! If you're going to look for trouble,
you found it!"

By the twelfth round, both men had tired. They clinched, heads ear
to ear, embracing,
then punching underneath, whaling away at the other's

ribs, face. Such
intimate hostility. As if, could they have spoken to each other
through plastic mouth guards,

they would have groaned out curses, endearments, pillow talk.
At the close of the sixth round
the Kid had landed a combination, ending in a hard right

to Emile's chin.
He had gone down in his corner for an eight count,
but got back up

and started slugging as the bell rang and delivered him
from an almost certain
knockout. The crowd had shouted, whistled, roared.

In the black-and-white footage
of the TV broadcast on YouTube, the referee Ruby Goldstein breaks up
their clinch. Photographers

lean in and slide their old-fashioned flashbulb cameras across the ring's
sweat-spattered
canvas floor to get a closer shot of the exhausted fighters. Cigarette

and cigar smoke
hangs heavy. The announcer Don Dunphy complains, "This is probably
the tamest round

of the entire fight." One second later Emile staggers the Kid
with an overhand right.
"Griffith rocks him." Emile lands twenty-nine punches in eighteen

seconds. "Paret against
the ropes, almost hopeless." Emile steps back, winds up, then swings
                    to get his full

body weight into each punch. Eyewitness Norman Mailer, ten feet
                    away from the fighters,
would write that Emile's right hand was "whipping like a piston rod

                    which had broken through
the crankcase, or like a baseball bat demolishing a pumpkin."
                    The crowd screams,

frenzied as piranhas stripping in less than half a minute the flesh
                    from a cow fallen
into the river. As Emile hammers the Kid's head with nine straight uppercuts

                    in two seconds, so it whips
back and forth in the slow-motion replay like a rag doll's head shaken
                    by a girl throwing

a tantrum, one commentator observes, "That's beautiful
                    camera work,
isn't it?" Another responds, "Yeah, terrific." While Emile mauls

                    the Kid with mechanical
precision, he may be thinking of how the Kid reached out
                    and tauntingly patted

his left buttock, lisping *Maricón, maricón,* as Emile stood
                    stripped-down
to his black trunks on the scales at the weigh-in. Or he may be thinking

of his job designing ladies'
hats in the Garment District. Attach that ostrich feather to the brim
                of the blue boater, left hook,

pile-driver right. Lean into the punch. Put him away. But Paret,
                tangled in the ropes,
won't go down. Clancy had told him to keep punching until

                the referee separated
them. Emile doesn't know that the Kid will never regain
                consciousness, will die

in ten days. He doesn't know that for the rest of his life
                he will have nightmares
in which he and Paret are marionettes. Someone jerks his strings. He can't

                stop punching. He will become
world champ four more times, but will himself be beaten almost
                to death by five young

homophobes, one with a baseball bat, as he leaves a gay bar near Port
                Authority. He will drive
a pink Lincoln Continental. After Paret's death, Manny

                Alfaro, the Kid's manager,
will say, "Now, I have to go find a new boy." His widow,
                Lucy, will bury him

in the St. Raymond Cemetery in the Bronx. She will never
                remarry, will tell an interviewer,
"Dream? I stopped dreaming a long time ago." Boxing matches

will stop being televised
for the next decade. Ruby Goldstein will referee only one more fight,
                    then retire. Emile

will suffer dementia pugilistica. He will be forced to sell his Continental
                    and will ride the bus,
he'll say, "like everyone else." Benny Paret, Jr., the Kid's son

                    who was two years old
when Emile killed his dad, will meet and forgive him forty-two years
                    later. Lucy

had refused to go to the Garden or watch the fight on TV.
                    A neighbor had to tell her.
Across nineteen million flickering screens nation-wide

                    they hoisted the Kid's
still body onto a stretcher and carried him slowly out of the ring.
                    Don Dunphy signed off,

"saying goodnight for your hosts, the Gillette Safety
                    Razor Co., makers
of the $1.95 Adjustable Razor, super blue blades, foamy shaving

                    cream, and Right Guard
Power Spray Deodorant, and El Producto, America's largest-selling
                    quality cigar."

Frozen Assets

"Plus ça change, plus c'est la même chose," my uncle Mart
                        liked to tell me
when I was eleven, he who had barely a dime to his name

                      but had read all of Proust
in French and would march around our house, arms swinging, singing
                        "Aux armes, citoyens,

Formez vos bataillons, Marchons, marchons!" I was never sure
                      what war he was fighting.
But now I know that he and Jean-Baptiste Alphonse Karr,

                      the nineteenth-century novelist
whom he was quoting, got it right. *The more it changes, the more*
                      it's the same damn thing.

Take, for instance, Diego Rivera's portable fresco, *Frozen*
                      Assets, painted
in 1932 on an eight-by-six-foot slab of reinforced cement

                      in a galvanized steel
framework for his solo show at the newly-opened Museum
                      of Modern Art.

Diego rearranged the Manhattan skyscrapers so he could get
                      all those just-erected
or still-under-construction office buildings into the same

                      picture—Equitable
Trust, Empire State, Chrysler, McGraw-Hill, Daily News, Bank of Manhattan
                      Company Building,

and Rockefeller Center. The skyline of capitalism still glitters
                    with the marble dust
Diego mixed half-and-half with lime for the final coat of plaster

                    applied over
the "brown coat," which was laid down over the "scratch coat." I marvel
                    eighty years later

at the freshness of Rivera's colors, the blue-tinted McGraw-Hill Building,
                    the red-primed, rustproof
girders going up, I-beams lifted high by the meat hooks and steel cables

                    of derricks with yellow-latticed
arms. It was the height of the Great Depression. Three thousand four hundred
                    workers, most of whom

had been unemployed, built the 102-story Empire State, tallest
                    skyscraper in the world,
in one year and forty-five days. The riveters worked in teams

                    of four. The "passer"
heated ten rivets at a time in a small forge, then threw them red-hot
                    one by one

with tongs sometimes sixty feet or more to the "catcher"
                    perched on a girder.
He caught them in an old paint can, knocked them clean of cinders

                    against a beam,
and inserted them with his tongs into the girders' holes. The "bucker-up"
                    held them in place

while the "gunman" drove them home with a compressed-air hammer.
                    The hot metal fused
with the girders. The Empire State's last rivet was solid

                    gold. Hundreds
of minute commuters, faceless and all the same shade of brown,
                    jam the platform

on an elevated line and wait for the next downtown local in Rivera's
                    fresco. Below them
Diego shows us a cross section of the steel and glass shed

                    on the Municipal Pier
at East 25th St. There the homeless and unemployed sleep
                    in seven close rows

on mats under mercury-vapor lamps that turn them gray. They become
                    bodies in a morgue,
pupae shrouded in a gray cocoon, waiting to grow wings,

                    rip their way out,
fly free. Uncle Mart, my father's eldest brother, rarely held a steady
                    job, drifted

until he turned seventy, then worked as a sexton and church janitor.
                    Uncle Frank, the middle
brother, co-owned the Walsh-Platt Chrysler and Dodge Dealership.

                    Frank didn't want to be
seen with his "black sheep brother." One black-suited policeman keeps wary
                    watch over Rivera's sleepers.

Sixty blocks south from where I stand in the Museum of Modern Art,
            the Occupy Wall St.
protesters camp out in Zuccotti Park under

            Mark di Suvero's
Joie de Vivre, seventy-foot-tall red-girder man or woman
            with both arms upraised

in ecstasy or outrage. The crowd walks down Wall St., chanting
            "This is what
democracy looks like!" and "We are the 99%!" and

            "The people united
will never be defeated!" They wave their signs like wings, flock
            of ragged migrant monarchs

or great spangled fritillaries. Their wings say, WALL ST. IS WAR ST.
            Jail The Banksters
EAT THE RICH   I'm So Angry I Made A Sign   HYDROFRACKING

            3-9 MILLION GALLONS
PER WELL   1000s OF WELLS   100s OF TOXIC CHEMICALS
            CALL GOV.   SAY "NO!"

One man and two women in baggy, polka-dotted jumpsuits and orange wigs,
            faces painted white
and streaming large blue tears, carry two banners—CLOWNS

            AGAINST CAPITALISM
and THIS IS THE DAWNING OF THE AGE OF HILARIOUS
            OCCUPY EVERYTHING.

Other clowns blow reveille on trumpets, bang bongos. WAKE UP
                    SHIFT HAPPENS.
On the third-story balconies above them, men in blue blazers

                    and women in golden
pantsuits lean on the railings, sip flutes of champagne, video the crowd
                    with their smart phones,

ironically raise their glasses to the protesters, smile. The crowd shouts
                    "Banks got bailed out!
We got sold out!" The policemen move them on. *Plus ça change,*

                    plus c'est la même
chose. My father let Mart live with us for several years when there
                    was nowhere else

for him to go. He pruned the euonymus and spirea hedges, cut down
                    dead trees, sawed,
split, stacked cordwood. He planted daffodils, azaleas, day lilies,

                    and gold chrysanthemums,
taught the poor soil to flower. Underneath the homeless sleepers, Rivera
                    has cut away the asphalt

to reveal the network of sewage and water pipes, electrical conduits
                    that feed the city.
The bottom layer of the fresco shows an underground, steel-barred

                    bank vault guarded
by an expressionless policeman who looks straight through us. Diego
                    modeled it on the vaults

---

he saw at One Wall Street in the Irving Trust Building, which also rises
                in his fresco's skyline.
The walk-in safe with a spoked wheel to open its massive door

                stands shut. Behind the grille
a woman in a gray dress and high heels sits at a table and fondles
                a necklace of gold

medallions, which she has taken from her safe-deposit box. This whole
                city rests
on greed's bedrock. In the earth-colored waiting room

                a clerk who resembles
John D. Rockefeller, Sr. pours over a list of assets at a desk covered
                with a green blotter. Two women

in fur-collared coats and fishnet stockings wait on a bench with a man
                who holds his derby
in his lap and has the jowly jaws and round spectacles of John

                D. Rockefeller, Jr.
They all want to ogle their safe-deposit boxes. Keep the wealth
                within the family.

Mart would march ten miles a day on our icy winter
                back roads in an unlined
trench coat. "I've got to keep moving," he spat out. "Don't freeze

                your assets, though
you freeze your ass off!" Half crazy, surviving on black coffee
                and apple pie at luncheonette

counters, my uncle kept tramping the frozen slush, fulminated against
                      the two-party system.
Twenty years dead, he wakes among Diego's gray sleepers. "Ticktock,"

                      he whispers, "is how the world
goes. C'est toujours la même chose." He slams out our kitchen door,
                      tall and thin

as any Giacometti statue, pair of scissors walking. He strides in perpetual
                      motion, pendulum
loosed from a grandfather clock, ticktock toward the tumor that will

                      kill him. They'll remove
half his bowel. On his last postcard he'll scrawl, "The Nation's terminal . . .
                      and I've cancer of the *semi*-colon."

23 Quai de Voltaire

Walking east along the left bank
of the dirty, brown-green Seine, I look up and see on the gray-yellow
wall of a five-story

limestone apartment building a small, black-lettered plaque.
It's easy to translate.
"Rudolf Nureyev, 1938-1993, dancer and choreographer, Director

of the Paris Opéra
Ballet, lived in this house during the last years of his life." One life,
a little less

than fifty-five years, gets condensed into one short declarative
sentence, complete
with parenthetical dates, its three-item appositive, and two prepositional phrases,

one of place,
the other of time. No sinewy syntax, no elegant period
can contain

Nureyev's body. Nor hope to imitate his grands jetés, those pinwheeling
leaps in *Le Corsaire*
where, wearing a gold chain around his bare chest and over

his right shoulder,
plus golden harem pants, love's slave in high art's bondage, Nureyev
circled the stage

in eight great bounds—"that young lion," as Margot Fonteyn, his favorite partner,
liked to call him.
Watching him and his Danish ex-boyfriend, Erik Bruhn, dance together

in the film version
of *Romeo and Juliet* when I was ten taught me desire, though I didn't
know it then. I couldn't

look away from the bulge in his unjockstrapped crotch. In New York City bathhouses,
in the back rooms
of London tearooms and Paris gay bars, Nureyev fucked and got fucked by

his "butch boys"
while all the clientele watched. When he wanted to upstage another dancer, he would
"turn his back to the audience

and flex his butt. It worked every time," claimed one balletomane.
Yet he never
acknowledged publicly he was gay, though he told Mike Wallace in an interview

"I know what it is
to make love as a man and a woman." Death outed him. HIV-positive
for his last twelve years, he kept

dancing through weight loss, fevers, night sweats, pneumonia, hepatitis,
injections of HPA-23,
AZT, good days, bad days. Danseur noble, he never

mentioned AIDS
or age. His technique deteriorated. The audience booed. He directed the final dress
rehearsals of *La Bayadère*,

the only classic ballet he'd never danced in the West,
lying down.
"La machine est cassée," he remarked to a friend. The machine is

---

broken. On opening night
he lay on a couch in a gilded box on the left-hand side of the Garnier's stage, dressed
in scarlet satin.

He sipped champagne. Afterward, backstage, they gave him the Legion of Honor.
The scarlet satin
made his face gaunter, more haunted. He did not weep.

He had already
wept. "Can you imagine," he said, sweeping one arm diagonally from the footlights
to the upper balconies

as he used to do in his grand bows encore after encore, "I am going
to have to say good-bye
to all this!" He was no sentimentalist. But it was, of course,

curtains—
"Ciao, bellissimo!" "See you later, alligator." "Tassie-la-la."
Good-bye

to 23 Quai de Voltaire, to the view from his overheated apartment
of the south side of the Louvre,
its black roofs with round windows like portholes. Good-bye to the Seine

flowing slowly
with its cargo of litter, its *bateaux-mouches* full of drunk Americans every August.
Good-bye to the plane trees

wearing only ragged bark and diaphanous green leaves. Their white arms sway
in the light breeze,
the street's corps de ballet. Good-bye to the booksellers shutting

                    their green vending stalls,
locking up at dusk the books of dangerous, perverted, French poets—Verlaine, Rimbaud,
                    and Jacques Prévert—

along with cheap posters of Moulin Rouge dancers, collector's editions
                    of the first *Playboy*
still sheathed in plastic, and reproductions of sepia

                    pornographic postcards,
Rubensesque beauties with un-retouched, lush, pubic muffs. Who would have thought in 1894
                    that pornography could become

nostalgic? Good-bye to the boulevard boys on rollerblades, whose tight shorts
                    barely cover
their muscled asses. Nureyev still wanted to fondle that rapturous

                    flesh. Good-bye
to the one-man jazz band on the corner of Rue de Beaune, the guy whose left foot
                    keeps the beat

on a high hat's sizzling cymbals, whose right foot improvises
                    doom's dumb boom
on the big bass drum, while his left hand plays a wheezing accordion

                    and his right alternates
trumpet and trombone. He's giving us his own poor version
                    of "My Favorite Things."

Sad schmaltz. Nureyev said good-bye to the night and the day.
                    So long,
long schlong! But what I see when I read the small

sign that says
Nureyev lived his last years here behind the tall locked black doors with their
spit-polished brass handles

is him young again on Yonge Street, Toronto's gay district,
at two a.m.,
after several opening night parties, his first North American tour,

dancing like
an ouzo-crazed matador between the swerving cars in time to their syncopated
honking. What cabrioles,

what tours jetés, glissades, grands changements de pieds, what fouettés
did he do
weaving back and forth through that moving traffic? He screamed at the police,

"You cannot arrest me.
I am Rudolf Nureyev!" "Yeah, smart ass?" one cop replied. "And I'm Fred Astaire.
Let's go. Get in the goddamn car!"

Christ's Entry into Brussels in 1889

When I pick up my ninety-year-old father-in-law to drive him
                    to the early service
at Galilee Episcopal Church, where he has gone for the last quarter

                century, he hobbles
out through the two automatic doors of the retirement home
                on his flimsy wood

cane. He has lost weight so his blue suit hangs loosely around
                    his stooped frame.
He has smeared on his cracked lips the white cream that Dana, my wife

                and his daughter, has given him
so he looks like James Ensor's grinning white-faced death's-head
                with lipless mouth

and a black top hat partially wrapped in green crepe paper
                in the lower left corner
of the oil painting *Christ's Entry into Brussels in 1889.*

                The fourteen-by-six-foot
canvas shows a carnivalesque parade of partygoers—
                caricatures of Ensor's

acquaintances, relatives, and enemies—all marching down a boulevard
                to celebrate
Christ's second coming. The small haloed figure of Christ,

                who rides a donkey
and is a self-portrait of Ensor, is lost in the crowd of masked,
                mugging, guffawing

or unmasked, leering, squinting faces. They carry banners and placards,
             some later painted over
by Ensor, that announce VIVE LA SOCIALE (Long Live the Socialist State),

             FANFARES DOCTRINAIRES
TOUJOURS REUSSI (Doctrinaire Fanfares Always Succeed), LES CHARCUTIERS
             DE JERUSALEM

(The Butchers of Jerusalem), and COLMAN'S MUSTART
             (Colman's Mustard).
None too subtly, Ensor implies that if Christ came back, we

             would co-opt
the miracle to promote our own agendas—political reforms,
             businesses,

product advertisements. Christ would be ignored. When Erwin
             and I enter
his church, the well-dressed parishioners who presumably know him

             turn away.
They don't want to associate with an old, dying man whose suit
             is unpressed and stained,

as I now notice, with brown spots that might be splattered tomato sauce.
             I want to rise up
from my pew and shout, "Fuck you, frozen chosen!" So what

             if only yesterday
Erwin, after a long phone conversation about his Volvo which had failed
             its annual inspection

and has to have new tires and brakes, asked me, "Don't I know you
                    from somewhere?
What's the name of your organization?" Momentarily shocked,

                    I opted
for the flip rejoinder—"My organization is codenamed DANA."
                    I want to explain to everyone

that he's only an old man with Parkinson's and mild dementia
                    who is trying to brave out
his last days and go to church as if nothing untoward

                    is happening
to him. We listen to the gospel in which a disciple
                    tells Christ, mobbed

by his followers, "Your mother and your brothers
                    are outside, asking
for you." He replies, "Who is my mother? Who are my brothers?"

                    and gestures to the crowd,
"Here are my mother and my brothers. Whoever does the will
                    of God is my brother,

my sister, my mother." Everyone around us nods sagely, but keeps
                    everyone else
at arm's distance, pretends Erwin and I and death itself

                    are invisible. In his sermon
the priest says that Christ was liar, lunatic, or Lord—
                    the only three

logical, mutually exclusive, alternatives. "But why can't he
                    be all three,"
I want to ask him, "just as Erwin is your father and brother

                    and a doddering
old man unrelated to you?" In Ensor's canvas, the mayor perches
                    on a reviewing stand

next to a clown in orange and blue pants, who bends over
                    to show us
his large ass. Ensor's people have bulbous noses, crossed eyes,

                    and bloated cheeks.
They gossip, fart, curse. Their faces are Halloween masks of lust,
                    greed, gluttony,

hypocrisy. A man and woman suck each other's tongues
                    like pink popsicles.
Emile Littré, atheist social reformer with a red-brown bird's nest

                    of a beard and a drunkard's
red nose, wears a bishop's miter, waves a drum major's baton,
                    leads the rabble

forward. Why should I expect anything different outside
                    Ensor's great
painting? One erased placard said of *Les XX*, the group of artists

                    who refused to exhibit
this picture: LES VIVISECTEURS BELGES INSENSIBLES
                    (Hardhearted Belgian

Vivisectors). Ensor knew firsthand that to be ignored is to be
                    cut open while still
alive and then eviscerated. Next to the top-hatted death's-head

                    a big-mouthed clown
frowns. The man with wiry black hair laughs. A military brass band
                    marches ahead of Christ,

drowns out whatever he has to say. The bandleader's khaki shirt
                    is studded with war medals.
Erwin and I are part of this parade. We too are entering

                    Brussels, City of the Second
Coming. Only one gray-haired man stops to wish Erwin well
                    when he leaves

the church, shuffling through the dark double doors into sun.
                    I hold his hand
like that of a child too young to cross the street by himself.

                    His fingers are rough,
warm, clumsy. It's like holding a lump of dried clay. I tell him when
                    he has to step down.

One Page Torn from the Book of the Names of the Dead

I'm walking on the dead, treading them down to
nothing but the crackling scraps of fiery leaves I

kick to extinguish them. *Urbin Fiers   Bertha
Dick   Mykola Markovsky   Pieter Ombregt*

Margaret Menino. I read yesterday
their handwritten names on one page of the Book

of the Names of the Dead that rested on a
lectern near Our Lady of Guadalupe

clothed in her blue-green mantle and hood studded
with stars. She was standing on the black horn of

a new moon, borne on the strong, peasant shoulders
of Juan Diego, who saw the sixteen-year-old

virgin in a vision in the desert near
the hill of Tepeyac. *Rhiannon McCuish*

*Joseph Onorato   Connie Ries   Victor
Yew Wei Sii   Clearence Croy.* The dead are always

with us. My father bends over the chessboard,
three moves ahead of me, slides his black rook, says

"Check." I jump my knight from F3 to D2
to shelter my king, avoid checkmate. He smiles

at how well he's taught me. Know your opponent's
mind, all the moves he can make, how you'll answer

each one. In the Book of the Names of the Dead
I wrote his name to honor and exorcise

him. Good ghost, be with me. Stay away. You have
possessed me. Now I disown you, must stamp out

the sparks of leaves that are your ashes, grind them
to compost beneath the heels of my mule-hide

boots. You are disintegrating into dirt,
layer after layer. *Julie Branson   Claire*

Crider   Mary Tang   Rosemary Knowles   Penny
Park—pray for me, though you don't know me, and I

will pray to Our Lady of Guadalupe
that she may intercede for you whoever

and wherever you are. I wrote my mother-
in-law's name in the Book, she who had died from

Stage IV lung cancer, who once taught me to make
a wild-rice salad with halved red grapes, cherry

tomatoes, golden raisins, toasted slivered
almonds, artichoke hearts, hearts of palm, all dressed

with lemon juice, ground pepper, cold-pressed olive
oil. Feed me again. Strengthen my bones, dead mother.

Dead father, walk with me through these autumn streets
under the changing leaves' golden mosaics

that come ruining down until all that's left
is the bare vaulted nave of sky. Hosanna

of wind through black branches. *Dorothy Philpot*
Michael Kral   Carmen O de Nava   Edgar

Adriatico   Hope Lynch, you who have walked
on, let me be Soutine's *Man Praying*. That canvas

in flames is kiln for the black-suited figure
with hands together. Earthen vessel that must

be fired to bear water. His head is bald gold
skull. His hands emerge from the sleeves' black wicks,

flicker like fire. He's a candle guttering
in the winds of a firestorm. Whatever words

he prays, let me say them too. I keep repeating
the names of the dead to appease them, console

myself. They made it through this life, now know what
we crave and are afraid to know. Nothingness

gives suck to us. *Casmiro Santiago*
Kathleen Brune   Phyllis Sobotta   Grandpa Joe

Richard Zazmierczak, dip your fingers into
nothingness's river, asperge us with those

waters. *Anne Zord*—mother of all alphabets,
A through Z—help me to utter the names of

the dead and the living, to gather roses
and ragweed in winter, like Juan Diego,

carry them home in my cloak, open it to
find your image emblazoned there—a woman

radiating tongues of fire. Everyone the sun
touches burns. Silence, final word, sear my mouth.

La Playa los Muertos

Puerto Vallarta, Mexico

I.

Everyone comes to swim at la Playa los Muertos, the beach of the dead

No, more often than not, we come to sit in the hammock-like, blue-red-and-yellow-striped, cloth beach chairs under the blue sun umbrellas or the thatched palapas and sip margaritas from chilled, salt-rimmed glasses with chasers of beer

The waiters dress in white, are young and slender

We come to eat *mariscos*—tostadas with ceviche, shrimp enchiladas, octopus soup, mahi-mahi grilled in banana leaves with pineapple salsa. We watch the oiled girls in Rio bikinis and boys in thongs walk by on the beach of the dead

We say *Hola* and *Gracias* and point to what we want on the menu, unsure of how to pronounce it

The exchange rate is fifteen pesos to the dollar

We come to listen to the rough music the waves make all afternoon, both monotonous and infinitely various. We come to forget wherever it is we've come from

*

We watch the local men fish from the pier. Though they catch nothing, they discuss it at great length, trilling their r's and breathing out their long vowels through parted lips

I take my first picture of the day

I order coconut milk. The waiter brings it in the yellow-green husk whose top he has sliced
    off with a machete

He sticks a straw through the small hole so that I can sip it

It is lukewarm breast milk from tall trees with palm fronds

I write in a notebook

When I have finished drinking, the waiter cuts the coconut in half on scarred butcher block
    so that I can dig out the meat from the inner shell with a knife and eat

I pay in pastel paper currency printed with pictures of sun gods, conquistadors, and
    liberators

*

Two days ago I took snapshots of the one-room houses of the very poor, on whose flat
    roofs rainbows of laundry hang from baling twine

Because the poor have no front yards, their dogs sleep on those roofs, growl, and bark at
    passersby

I have walked on, with or without dropping coins into the tin can of the man without arms,
    who sits on the steps of the Church of Our Lady of Guadalupe

A cardboard sign strung by a string around his neck

Black lettering I don't understand

He calls out, *Ore por mí*

There are no beggars on the beach of the dead. The *policía* keep them away

Men hawk plastic bags of green, white, and pink cotton candy tied to ten-foot poles

*

My fourteen-year-old daughter has been vomiting for two days from flu or from eating bad
    chorizo tostadas and stays in our hotel room with the curtains drawn

She does not see, smell, or hear what I do on the beach of the dead or on the Malecón, stone
    boardwalk which winds like a serpent between boutiques and ATMs on one side and
    on the other the ocean flashing like broken glass

She watches *House* on TV

Dr. House limps around on his cane, diagnosing impossibly rare diseases, saving lives, and
    being willfully and wittily rude to everyone without exception

House, on forced clinic duty, tells his busty boss, Dr. Cuddy, "So either I can continue to
    swab people's privates or I can figure out if this guy's delirium, pain, and insanely
    high heart rate are life-threatening or just a personality quirk"

He makes my sick daughter laugh

*

On the beach of the dead, a Mexican family on vacation tosses a volleyball back and forth
    from grandmother to granddaughter to uncle to father to aunt to sister to mother to
    brother to grandfather

A girl throws sand at her older brother, who sprints as fast as he can from her

Two women jog four times up and down the steep stone stairs that zigzag from the
    mountaintop hotels to the beach. One shouts to the other in English, "Yes, there
    are 206 steps"

Sweat makes dark continents on the backs of their blue T-shirts

Now the brother holds the sister down on her back and shampoos her long tangled brown
     hair with sand. He laughs so hard he drools. She laughs from the pure exhilaration
     of finally getting her brother to notice her

                                        *

Today a bride and groom get their photograph taken, standing on the hot sand

She wears a white satin strapless gown and clutches to her breasts a bouquet of roses

He's in a black tux

The photographer disappears under his three-legged camera's black shawl

Click, and the shutter will catch the silent wave behind them, about to break, come crashing
     down

                                        *

A wrinkled woman, hair dyed blonde, wearing a green gauzy dress, floppy-brimmed
     straw hat, and onyx earrings, walks her dog on the beach of the dead

Her bloodshot blue eyes underscored with kohl

The dog too is ancient and has lost all its hair except for several stray, white, cotton-candy-
     like wisps. Its piebald hide is black with a few gray spots

Impossible to tell what breed, though now I notice the pink-gray teats

The old woman is speaking Spanish on her red cell phone

Her depilated dog meets a large greyhound pup, whose coat has the color, luster, and
     softness of pussy willows in April

They sniff each other, tails wagging like windshield wipers turned to intermittent, then to high

They play together, romp, cavort across the beach of the dead, kick sand over the lotioned, bronzed bellies of the sunbathers

Mathilda, venga aquí! shout the greyhound's owners

A big-bellied father gets buried in the sand by his children and then rises with a roar from the dead to run after the shrieking kids

*

Now the waiters from Spiaggia, the oceanfront restaurant that the wedding party has rented for the day, bring out overstuffed armchairs, polished mahogany coffee tables, tiki torches, and microphones and set them in the sand

It is as if a living room has been set up on the beach of the dead, as if a house has been turned inside out

A mariachi band comes out of the restaurant—four violinists, two trumpet players, four guitarists, and one singer. They form a horseshoe around the bridal couple, their friends, and relatives, who all talk at once and hold flutes of champagne like lit candles in front of them

No one will sleep tonight

*

Spiaggia, in Italian, means *beach* or *shore*

Spiegare means *explain, spread, unfold, unfurl*

Would that my sentences would *unfurl* like the blue and white silk banners hung over the streets of small dusty Mexican towns in celebration of the feast day of Our Lady of Guadalupe

The waves *unfold* on the *shore*

Spiaggia

Spiega

"'Splain that to me again," said my friend back in Carrollton, Georgia

Carrollton, named after Charles Carroll, the only Catholic signer of the Declaration of Independence and the longest-lived signer, dying at 97

Carol town

Signer

Singer

*

The mariachi men wear tight beige pants and jackets trimmed with metallic gold, matching straw sombreros

The singer sings, *Negrita de mis pesares,   Ojos de papel volando*

I ask the old woman with the dog what the words mean

Little negress of my sorrows, she says

Eyes like paper flying

One huge wave runs up the shore, laps at the singer's white and black, lizard-skin cowboy
     boots. He jumps back. Everyone laughs. He moves the microphone farther from
     the ocean

The wave leaves its signature on the dry sand

Put the mic close to the surf, I want to say, so we hear the ocean's slow breathing amplified

*

I stroll past the muscled bodies of the young men lolling in pairs on white towels on the gay
     section of the beach of the dead

The white towels shine in the noon sun and set off the men's black hair, moussed and spiky
     à la the latest fashion, their black eyes, and their skin the color of unglazed red-
     brown clay that has been fired all night and is still cooling in the kiln come morning

Their beauty makes me lower my eyes, ashamed of my own desire

I try to stay out of the sun

I cover my fifty-year-old body with an x-tra large gray T-shirt that says in faded black letters
     PURDUE BASEBALL

*

I wear baggy yellow swim trunks with one white stripe flanked by two blue ones down each
     side

My beige baseball cap's logo reads NICK'S above a black fish skeleton, under which is
     printed in smaller lettering, *Virginia Beach, VA*

It is useless to pretend that I am not an American

I am just another queer gringo on la Playa los Muertos

*

A corpulent man my age with his hair dyed a carefully restrained shade of auburn claps a
      waiter on the shoulder and says in English, "My, Juanito, but aren't you looking good
      today"

"Sí, Señor. What would you like to drink"

The fat man leaves large tips, bright brass and silver coins embossed with serpents and
      winged creatures

*

A young man holding a five-foot iguana goes from beach chair to beach chair, asking the
      turistas if they would like to take its picture with their digital cameras

The iguana has bright red spikes like coarse dune grass sticking up along its spine. Its
      orangey-brown scales form a beadwork highlighted by occasional green scales. On
      each side of its jowls, it has a round bulging plate the size of a twenty-peso piece,
      subtympanic shield which has no biological function. A wrinkled, leathery dewlap of
      scaly skin dangles from its chin like a beard. Each leg has five long toes that remind
      me of a child's curling fingers

Its eyes, black pinpoints against amber, stare back at me

The skin hangs loose around its legs, baggy trousers several sizes too big

Those unblinking eyes look back across millennia

O to be an ancient iguana held in a young man's warm arms, to be his livelihood, to be
      marveled over

*

A woman in a green bikini stands in the waves that break on la Playa los Muertos, reading a
  paperback. What dark, shining, salt-stained words are written there that she does not
  look up at the sun rising over the tall green mountains behind us

A fire-eater breathes out flames on the Malecón so that everyone stands back and claps

A man pisses circumspectly against a far wall, golden urine pooling at his feet before it sinks
  into the sand

The old people with their ropy legs and arms whose flesh hangs down like turkey wattles,
  they come in their white terry-cloth robes to sit in the sun

*

They have the thin wooden wrists of scarecrows

They wait to lie down on the massage table that stands like a bier in the shade cast by a white
  canopy

They wait for the masseur with his thick fingers

To pound, thump, and drub the blood back into their slack muscles

They moan again and again, as if he were making love to them

*

Those who have been dead come alive again on the beach of the dead

They sit on the bronze knees of the statues who meditate in a semicircle halfway down the
  Malecón and who gaze out blindly over the blinding waters of the Bahía de Banderas

*

I sit on the burnished lap of a robed woman who wears a deep-sea diver's helmet and has
      three long wavery tentacles emerging through holes in her helmet like thoughts from
      her left parietal lobe

The blue-green bronze of her round breasts has been touched to gold by countless hands

Dana, my wife, sits on the knees of a king with crossed arms, who has the head of a bird
      with a beak like a trumpet

I take their picture

They will remain undeveloped for years on the small, tightly wound scroll of dark film

*

We switch thrones

Play musical chairs

Now I move to a bronze bench that rests on two bronze human legs

Everyone must go around the semicircle

Each leg has two feet, heels together, pointing in opposite directions like a ballerina's in first
      position

Along the four edges of the bench have been carved and cast twenty staring eyes

Passerby, stop, sit, and look around you

Lean back against one of the bench's two huge bronze ears

Hear the gulls' cries mix with the surf, which is the voice of the invisible woman who sits
    next to you and wraps her arms around you in the same way that the warm air
    embraces you. It is scented with sea salt and, ever so slightly, with the purple
    bougainvillea growing from ten flower boxes on each of the five levels of the white
    spiral parking garage across the deserted Paseo Díaz Ordaz

You must see in twenty different directions at once

II.

A young man on the beach by the Malecón balances tall boulders, end to end, one
    impossibly atop another

He strains and sweats to lift stones the size of overgrown children

He cradles them in his arms, breathes hard

He stacks the cairns slightly askew so that they look like they will fall if the wind breathes the
    wrong way

Two or three stones to each cairn

One has four

They have the spare abstract beauty of late Brancusi sculptures

On the edge of the Malecón he has put a large white styrofoam cup, into which the crowd
    that watches him drops pesos

Three bronze dolphins leap and curve around each other in the midst of the mist from a
    circular, green-tiled fountain beneath palm trees, whose lower trunks have been
    painted white so it looks as if the trees are wearing white knee-high socks like
    schoolgirls

A twenty-foot bronze ladder extends upward from the Malecón at an eighty-degree angle

It ends abruptly, leads nowhere

Two bronze figures in pleated gowns with heads that are downward-pointing equilateral
    triangles, the shape of spanakopita, climb the ladder

Each stretches his right hand toward some invisible thing that only he sees in the sky, blue
    blackboard smudged with the chalk dust of a few cirrus clouds

The locals call the sculpture "Jacob's Ladder"

At the foot of the ladder, Jacob—same triangular head as the angels—stands with his mouth
    open in an O and raises both arms upward

He looks at the angels climbing the ladder to nowhere

His left foot rests on a pink-speckled boulder

In the Bible, Jacob laid his head on a pillow of stone to dream of angels

No, all night he has wrestled stones that are angels, pinned them to the cold sand that will
    turn hot when the sun rises

*

The rock-stacker wears baggy black pants rolled up to just below his knees

He is stripped to the waist, skin the color of Brazil nuts, curly black hair, a white shell
    necklace

One of his seven cairns suddenly topples

His bare left foot has a white bandage where a boulder has fallen on his instep

Working on a three-boulder cairn, he twists the huge top stone back and forth, trying to find
the right spot where the axes of the boulders will come into alignment

It is trial and error, tuning these stones to each other so they will stand

Sweat glistens on his thick black eyebrows and runs into his eyes

He has to squint

He finds the right place for his stone and steps back

Three stones stand on each other's shoulders—yellow, gray, lavender

Everyone claps, tosses more pesos into his cup

Another cairn falls

*

Dana and I make love in the late afternoon

We are staying at the Hotel El Pescador, the Fisherman

A hummingbird, no larger than a child's thumb, perches on the orangey-pink bougainvillea
climbing the wall outside our second-story balcony

*

Dana lets the white towel fall from around her breasts

Across her abdomen: five small red moles called cherry angiomas, known medically as
Campbell de Morgan spots, benign

As if someone has scattered there a few grains of cayenne pepper

*

The hummingbird's green wings, now still and folded, resemble the leaves of the
     bougainvillea

Now its wings make a green blur

It is like one of the battery-powered, hand-held "personal fans" we used to buy at
     amusement parks in Georgia in the summer

*

We would direct the air from those one-inch-long fan blades toward whatever part of our
     bodies was sweatiest

It felt like someone blowing on elbow, cheek, clavicle

"I want to be in charge of the next kiss," says Dana

*

Her tongue roves slowly over the roof of my mouth, tongue, the insides of my cheeks, teeth

She tastes of what we have eaten

Scallions, garlic

Almonds

*

Sometimes I think her long tongue almost touches my epiglottis

At sunset the sky blooms

It is the color of the bougainvillea outside our window in full flame

It never rains in the high season

*

When I fell in love with Dana twenty-four years ago, she had a spastic, gray Maine coon cat
    named Brip

"Brrrippp" was the sound she trilled at the torn screen door to call him inside for his dinner

His name in her mouth was the sound of worn blue cotton pajamas being ripped up for rags

Because Brip ate dry cat chow called "Fisherman's Medley," Dana nicknamed him "the Little
    Fisherman"

The hummingbird's needle-nose beak drills nectar from each fragile cup

*

Let the sun close its one fiery blossom

Let the golden script of cirrus clouds blow away like so much chaff above the blue Bahía de
    Banderas in the high season

Bahía de Banderas, bay of flags flying—red, green, yellow, orange, pink, purple, sky blue, sea
    blue—hundreds of them strung on ropes across narrow streets in the old city

*

In the morning the maid puts fresh sheets on our beds, changes the towels, gives us new
    rolls of toilet paper

A young man mops the terra-cotta tiles of the hotel lobby with a mop that looks like gray
    dreadlocks

A ten-year-old boy in red pants jumps down four stairs at once, arms outstretched, shouting
      "Wishhh," pretending to fly

Hotel porters hurry by with their dollies stacked six feet high with the pastel lozenges of
      luggage—white, pink, mint-green, azure, bright yellow

*

When the speedboat pulling the parasail turns away from us, I can read the black letters of
      the advertisement on the white chute, under which a woman dangles

AGUA—The Strip & Lingerie Club

Dana and I point upward and laugh, but sex *is* water

The woman's cries grow smaller

III.

The waves keep breaking on the shore of the dead all night

Their long repeated lament, *ai, ai,* as if the Pacific Ocean—the tranquil one—were saying
      Kaddish for each one of us

Or is the surf our mother's lullaby, easing each of us back to dreamlessness

No, the surf is a diamond-tipped needle stuck on static, the black grooves of a long-playing
      record

Dance music to which our parents used to jitterbug until dawn

Waves our grandparents would waltz to

The lights of the great hotels lining the dark mountains behind and to the north of the beach
of the dead shine all night

*

Tropicana, Yasmín, Gaviota Vallarta, Hacienda San Angel, Posada de Roger, Rosita, Casa
Dulce Vida, Ana Liz, Buenaventura—their lights do not go out

The night watchmen with their small black boxes of keys, hung over their shoulders on
leather straps, keep walking the hotel corridors, inserting the keys into locks on each
floor, in the lobby, by the pool to tell someone they've been there and have not
fallen asleep

*

Two late-night revelers stagger home to their hotel at 6 a.m., walking in the light surf along la
Playa los Muertos

I sit on our hotel's terra cotta-tiled terrace overlooking the Bahía de Banderas in the darkness

They wave at me, raise their almost empty bottles of tequila blanco to toast the dawn, which
is now only the slightest fading of the black sky

The east turns slowly to new, blue, unwashed denim

Silver rivets of stars

The man in the white thong, who is bald and has Kaposi lesions, has come early to walk the
beach of the dead and see the twilit dawn

He leans gently on his lover, as he would a crumbling stucco wall

Night still surrounds us, the color of black pottery from Oaxaca, fired in open pits at low
temperatures so that the wood smoke imparts its color to the clay

All of a sudden, sun

Comes up behind me like a mugger

The terra-cotta tiles turn in ten seconds from gray to pink, to rose, to their true red-earth
    tone

I turn

I turn and see the banks of layered altocumulus over the mountains glow the same color as
    the terra-cotta tiles under my feet

*

The sun is a juggler in a yellow derby and red bodysuit on the Malecón

She juggles five orange balls at once

The day is the whiteface mime who points to the prettiest girl in the audience, mimes her
    curves like a potter shaping a vase from wet clay, puts one thumb and index finger in
    his mouth, and whistles silently

The purple morning glories by the pool at the Hotel El Pescador open

The halogen security lights shut off

*

The first joggers in gray sweats shuffle by

A man comes and sits on a white plastic chair fifty feet from me and smokes his first
    cigarette

Firefly glow of the cigarette tip as he pulls the smoke all the way into his lungs

Its slow fade as he exhales

Hand in hand, a man and a woman walk down the beach

On the hotel terrace a young man in a gray-hooded sweatshirt sweeps into a red-handled
    dustpan the night's leavings: cigarette butts, candy wrappers, white camellia
    blossoms, plastic forks

Seven pelicans fly in a diagonal line low over the water thirty feet from the surf, skim the
    surface on hovering wings

*

Now I can see the sign that tells us the "Condiciones Del Mar"

The green flag is for "Mar En Calma"

The yellow for "Precaución"

The red for "Peligroso"

The flag today is green. We will take the water taxi to Yelapa

In three days we will fly home to the ice storms of Indiana, which we left a week ago at three
    degrees above zero

I still have the cold I caught in Chicago

*

The palm fronds sway in the light breeze like old men doing t'ai chi, moving their arms
    slowly from side to side

High hawks circle on an updraft

Dust, trash, and camellia blossoms, the young man sweeps them from the terra-cotta tiles
    into the one pile

*

Purple-necked pigeons, heads bobbing as they walk, look for taco crumbs under the white
    plastic tables stamped with blue crowns above the logo "Corona Extra"

A rooster crows, church bells start ringing

Neither they nor the rooster will shut up

Its cry is someone trying to rip sheets of tin with his bare hands

I smell something cooking from the taco stand on the side street

Grilled shrimp for tostadas

The hotel boy skims bougainvillea petals off the pool's surface with a square of fine netting
    on a pole

What does he do with the purple-red petals but throw them away

*

The pigeons coo and chortle

One early fishing boat with a blue awning sets out for the horizon beyond the Bahía de
    Banderas

In the distance, to the south, I see the three green loaf-shaped islands with brown cliffs.
    They are called "Los Arcos"

El arco iris means "rainbow"

Iris's arch

Iris, messenger of the gods, slid down to earth on rainbows that were to her as waterslides
    are to us

Los Arcos

*

My job is simple and unending: say the names of everything on the beach of the dead

It can't be done

Some of the pigeons are gray, white, and black

Others are brown and white

All have pinkish claws that almost match the terrace's tiles

*

A slalom water-skier in an orange life jacket kicks up rooster tails behind a speedboat

How can it be that one day he will die

His single ski flashes in the sun

He leans back against the pull of the boat so that his right shoulder nearly grazes the water

*

I too will awake, step away from my body, leave this poem

*

MAN PRAYING

Up the beach, farther north along the horseshoe bay, the yellow ten-story walls of the Hotel
    Canto del Sol shine

They are the color of egg yolk

Dana calls me on my cell phone to tell me she needs Twinings English Breakfast Tea, skim
    milk, toilet paper, an English-language newspaper

Lucy has stopped vomiting

On the beach of the dead a father and a daughter hit a small black ball back and forth with
    ping-pong paddles

*

A black-haired woman in a yellow shirt and red sweat pants jogs along the beach with a
    water bottle swinging in one hand

Her hips sway and say

Hola, todo el mundo

Hola, father and grown son, you who draw up two blue lounge chairs to watch the waves,
    talk quietly, and then fall silent when she passes

Hola, dead pigeon, stiff in the sand where you finally fell, one wing sticking up like a black
    sail

Hola, boy made of bronze, naked except for the straw hat that dangles from the string
    around your neck and jounces on your back as you ride over invisible waves on a
    sea horse, your own jet ski, whose verdigris tail curls into a Fibonacci spiral

Hola, men at the pier, trying to attract customers for your water taxis, shouting in English,
    "Do you want to go to Yelapa"

The waves break, keep repeating the decades of their endless rosary

Hola, hola

*

A young girl in turquoise shorts runs shrieking into the waves of la Playa los Muertos

She jumps up and down, waves blindly at the sun with both arms as if it were a white, silver-spiked piñata, which she hits and breaks open with a stick on the Day of the Three Kings

Hola, Rosita

Hola, Estella

Every day the sun breaks and spills its light over the Bahía de Banderas

We are children down on our hands and knees, scrabbling for hard candy

We cannot hoard the light, eat it, or give it away

*

O watch and listen

Listen   watch   O   and

and   and   O   O

Listen O   watch and

*

Ghost crabs with their eyes mounted on antennae scuttle sideways, rearrange and anagrammatize bits of straw washed up at the high-tide line

They carry away the straw in white claws almost as big as the rest of their bodies

A little yellow truck, which looks like a steamroller, goes beep-beeping down the beach,
    sweeps up sand and rocks, but spits back only the sand

Lighthouse Digest Doomsday List

The days are one thousand
puzzle pieces. Shake the rest of them out of the box so they lie strewn
                    on the flimsy card table

in the rented beach house half a block from the ocean. The rain
                    sluices down. Nothing
to do, except wait for sun and work at the jigsaw my daughter

                    started, but didn't
finish. Lucy's assembled most of the pieces with straight edges
                    to make four sides

of a square necklace. Patricia, whose two daughters are almost the same age
                    as ours, fitted
more pieces together so that a lighthouse on stilts rises out of the water.

                    Its fourth-order Fresnel lens shines
from a cupola on top of a square, white, one-room house with a red tin roof,
                    attic dormers,

and a deck running around all four sides, fenced with a white railing,
                    balusters like matchsticks.
A sign facing shoreward says in white letters on plywood painted black:

                    HIGH VOLTAGE
CABLES CROSSING   DO NOT ANCHOR. I'd like to live there
                    away from everyone.

Far from my father-in-law dying slowly of Parkinson's,
                    his enlarged prostate
that won't let him urinate anymore, so he has to be catheterized.

                    They take the catheter
out, but do not monitor him closely enough. He's a liar,
                    ashamed of his body

breaking down. He won't tell anyone that he can't pee.
                    He's admitted
to the hospital with sepsis—high fever, low blood pressure, rising white

                    cell count—hallucinating.
He almost dies. Unaccountably, they put the Foley catheter in,
                    take it out,

put it in again, take it out again, can't make up their collective
                    medical minds—
those doctors with 'poor communication skills'—then put it back in

                    for good.
His penis is a pincushion. He wears a diaper. Somehow he
                    survives the week

on the step-down unit. The machines to which he's hooked up
                    bleat at him
every five seconds like a truck backing up. He tells me, "I hate

                    the way everyone
is always talking about my body. I don't exist anymore.
                    I'm just a vessel—

they measure my intake and output. So many milliliters
                    of water I drink
equal so many milliliters of urine." To be rid of the body

and its suffering,
I would live in a lighthouse on wooden spider legs in a jigsaw puzzle.
                    I would spend

the long summer days, when night holds off and doesn't fall until
                    9:30, watching
the shipping pass, that one-by-one parade of black-hulled

                    oil tankers
and container ships with cargo like brightly colored Legos
                    piled on their decks.

Keeper of my daddy-longlegs lighthouse, I would do interminable
                    unfinishable
jigsaw puzzles of lighthouses. Always there would be

                    one piece missing,
which I would search for on the floor, then under the couch
                    cushions. Slowly, over the next

two days, the puzzle picture emerges with its ragged interior
                    edges, wood veneer
of the card table showing through less and less. In the foreground, a painting

                    of lighthouses collaged
together. The 'New' Cape Henry Light, finished in 1881,
                    with its black and white

elongated rectangles like a harlequin's leg clad in diamond-patterned
                    tights, rises
through the fog with its light shining every fifteen seconds.

From the top of a yellow pole
on a trawler, whose hull is painted red, its smokestack and gantry
                    hoist yellow,

its suspended lifeboat white, another light pulses. They call it
                    a "lightvessel"
or "lightship." It is used in deep water. The puzzle's border

                    is formed by photographs
of thirty-two lighthouses. The Sharps Island Light, mounted
                    on a concrete caisson

that was damaged in 1977 by an ice floe, tilts fifteen degrees.
                    It looks like the Leaning
Tower of Pisa. It's included in the Lighthouse Digest Doomsday List

                    of endangered lighthouses.
I too list. My MRI in May showed spinal deterioration:
                    "a compressed disc,

disc dehydration, impressive ligament hypertrophy, severe
                    facet arthropathy,
marrow edema, two bulging discs." All these medical terms

                    I only half-understand
mean that I won't run ever again. I can't sit or stand straight without
                    pain. My remaining

days and years interlock. Gradually, the lighthouses of the Chesapeake,
                    whose names are listed
on the box, get pieced together—Old Point Comfort Light,

Thimble Shoal Light,
Wolf Trap Light, Point No Point. The names make their own
prose poem—Concord Point,

Bloody Point Bar, Hooper Strait Light, Solomons Lump.
Let the names keep shining.
This bit of shadow like a black lace tablecloth on water

goes under the screw piles
of that red lighthouse. A jigsaw can't be reasoned out; it's more
intuition, shape

to shape, color to color. One must match textures. I pick up
a piece of blue-gray fog
and look for that exact shade. Rag of tattered mist, it fits right here.

Playing Badminton with Eleanor

It all comes back—
my high lofting shot, which makes our daughter Eleanor
back-pedal toward

the baseline, the killer slam, the light tap bouncing the birdie
so it skims
the net and drops unhittable into the opposite forecourt.

I haven't played
in the forty years since I turned sixteen. But my right arm
remembers. When I volley

with Eleanor, home from Guatemala for Christmas, too thin,
I'm trading shot
for shot with my dead father. Again, he lunges for the shuttlecock,

lobs it over
my head, or whacks it back straight at me. I don't have time
to duck or bring

my racket up. The shuttle slams into my sternum. I clutch
my heart, pretend
I'm shot. My father, midcourt, my mother on the sideline

with my blank-eyed brother
not right in the head, Down syndrome, and I—all four of us—
die laughing.

I didn't know till now the dead keep playing badminton.
My father has the lightest
touch, can place the hardest shots—right, far corner to catch

me flatfooted
near the net. He winks and laughs. Summer sun hammers us. Here,
outside the gym, snow's

falling. Time is always double exposure. I'm the same age my father was
                        when we stopped
playing. Eleanor is twenty-two, is learning how to live

                        with her bipolar
condition, eat regularly, exercise, sleep well, do yoga, chart
                        her moods, take meds,

no drugs. I have to learn to worry less. But what father
                        doesn't worry
for his daughters? "Yes, but worry isn't love," my mother tells me—

                        now ninety-five years old—
when I telephone her every week. We share the worry gene. I can't forget
                        her compulsively

rolling invisible necklace beads of jade between her thumb and index finger
                        while I was growing up.
She had to care for my brother, who lived at home for forty-two

                        long years and never
could grow up. Every day she cooked his oatmeal, into which
                        she would purée

spinach, green beans, broccoli, whatever vegetable she had on hand,
                        blue vitamin pills,
beige-speckled pills of bone meal. Michael never learned

                        to chew. I can't
imagine what she felt. Despair, resignation, and finally
                        strange gratitude?

But Eleanor isn't Michael, I have to keep reminding myself.
                    While she's home
with us, Eleanor works the night shift at Jimmy John's

                    as a sandwich maker
to get some money together to go back to Guatemala
                    and apprentice

herself to local midwives. I quiz her on sandwiches.
                    "Number 17,"
I say, and she says, "Mayo, tomatoes, lettuce, cucumbers,

                    three scoops
of tuna, sprouts," as if it were a complex mathematical equation
                    to solve

the half-life of some radioactive isotope.
                    All I know
is joy. My daughter's come home. I'll see her every day

                    until she leaves again.
We'll play more badminton. She's learning to tap the fickle shuttlecock
                    just over the net

so that it drops where I can't possibly hit it back. I lunge,
                    miss, fall
to the hardwood court, limbs flailing in all four cardinal

                    directions. Eleanor
cracks up. I'm laughing with her at the absurdity of fathers. My own
                    dead father claps and claps.

Aubade with Foley Catheter

            Because I cannot sleep
through the whole night, I get up early to watch the sun
                come up out of the ocean

and listen to how the waves break in long lamenting iterations.
                What furious industry!
They swell, crest, crash, smash, hurl themselves upon the sand's

                flat ironing board
as if the surf has an infinity of fresh-washed laundry in blue hampers
                to press and starch

before the day is over. Each wave groans as it withdraws.
                Twenty-four-hour labor.
Perhaps the ocean is trying to give birth, contracting,

                resting, pushing,
panting. But no infant comes bawling forth unless
                it's this sun,

bald head slick with blood and the ocean's salt vernix. Hard birth of each
                new day. I watched
yesterday morning the nurse re-catheterize my father-in-law,

                rushed to the ER
two nights before with sepsis. He hugged his stomach like a pregnant woman
                and moaned. The nurse

swabbed the head of his penis with orange-brown disinfectant
                on a Q-tip.
She streaked his withered, gray cock—stalk that had planted my wife

and her two brothers in their
deceased mother's womb—with sunrise. The nurse inserted the plastic
                    tube into his penis,

and the three of us watched the catheter bag on the IV pole fill
                    with one and a half liters
of golden urine. "It's clear," the nurse said. "No infection."

                    Ninety-one-year-old Erwin
had survived another night. Because this is a poem, I could say the sun
                    rises out of the dark

Atlantic like the thin round wafer that my dead father,
                    priest of the Episcopal Church,
used to raise over his head in the belief God would descend

                    and inhabit that bread.
His acolyte, I could say sunrise is a white blinding peony
                    opening and never

wilting. It rises quarter inch by quarter inch. No, today the sun
                    is my father-in-law
Erwin Roeser's catheter bag shining endlessly with urine.

Like Jacob at Peniel

*And Jacob called the name of the place Peniel: for I have seen God
face to face, and my life is preserved.*

Genesis 32: 30

I too have wrestled
with God all night long, have breathed and bathed in his rank
body odor, that mixture

equal parts black dirt, grilled blood sausage, pine sawdust, gardenias,
and old, rain-stained
leather. Have felt his ribcage heave against mine, have rammed

my cheek hard
into the tender place between clavicle and neck, licked there
his salt sweat

like a man dying slowly of thirst in the rain shadow of the Gobi Desert.
I too have discovered his mirage
is an oasis green with the rustling of spikenard leaves, in whose spiked shade

I knelt, cupped clumsy
palms. I filled them to brimming with cool water that trembled and flashed
shards of sunlight, and at long last

drank. My chapped, cracked lips have kissed his nipples hard
as tulip buds about
to flower into flames. Like some fire-throated hummingbird, wings

beating fifty times
per second, I have sipped nectar there. We have struggled, thigh
to thigh, neither of us

winning or losing. He too has touched the hollow of my thigh
                    so that I wake
to pain shooting from my left buttock down the leg

                    to the two outer
toes gone completely numb. I cannot walk straight, limp
                    through the livelong

day. God said, *Let me go, for the day breaketh.* And I replied,
                    I will not let
thee go, except thou bless me. Then he said, *Behold,*

                    you shall love men
and women equally. You shall remain with the woman you love,
                    who has borne you

two beautiful daughters. You will lie down with her in the night season's
                    ecstasy. But you
shall also watch the young men, who have taken off their shirts

                    under the steady stare of the sun
so that their summer torsos resemble the sinewy tanned trunks of the Natchez crape
                    myrtle in full white blossom,

walk down the street and pass you by. Thus shall you be blessed.
                    And so loneliness
has become the stone on which I lay my head to sleep. Like Jacob

                    I dream
a ladder up to heaven and naked men like angels ascending
                    and descending,

the C major scale a harpist's fingers play upon a harp with golden strings.
They are always
young angels, broad backs tattooed with blue herons of fire. I hear

the thrum of their burning
wings lift them up. Come morning, they are gone. Only the stone
I've slept on.

Fugitive Pigment

Winslow Homer's sable
bristle brush dipped and gently tinted with red lake
the glistening

muscles of the diver's back as he gripped the stern
of a white rowboat
with his right hand and pulled himself half out of water.

His left hand raised
the red sponge he dove twenty feet through ocean luminous
as Chartres' blue

stained glass to harvest, holding his breath for a full minute
until he felt
his lungs almost explode and broke the surface. His beautiful

back is turned
to us. His name is lost. The artist's desire is still
spelled out

in the way light flows and streams off that broad black back,
in how the white hull
ripples with sunlight. Red lake is a "fugitive

pigment,"
meaning that it fades quickly when exposed
to light,

humidity, and air pollutants. We will never see
Winslow Homer's
black Bahaman sponge diver the way he painted him

in 1898,
watercolor on cream wove paper. Haze of sky
is a flat wash.

Beyond the horseshoe bay's low promontory and yellow
sliver of far
beach, what might be a lighthouse or mast. The two palm trees

look like windmills.
A distant sail's right triangle. Dark parallelogram of a stowed
oar's blade sticks up

over the gunwale. That's all it is or was—one casual
moment lifted,
hefted, held. The bold brushstrokes have turned

fugitive,
dimmed to taupe. After two months, Winslow went back
to Maine,

Prouts Neck, old age, to paint a colder coast.
He matted and framed
the sponge diver, hung him on a guest room's wall. Where the mat

overlapped and covered
the watercolor's left, right, and lower edges, the pigment
did not fade. Years later

some museum curator would strip off the gray mat, discover
his original magentas—
red lake for wave shadows, for the diver's coccyx, for the red-purple

       coral reef
underneath the undulating, ever-changing sheen
              of a Caribbean

so blue it might be sky swept clean by late summer
              hurricanes. Four
centimeters of undiminished waters frame what got washed away.

The *Davydov*

              The sadness one millimeter
under my psychotherapist's voice seems always about to break through
              like the first strident notes

of Elgar's Cello Concerto in E minor. Dave had to cancel
              our last session. He left me
a voicemail fifteen minutes before we were supposed to meet

              to say that his wife,
Rebecca, "was at a work event and had started projectile
              vomiting." He wanted

to go home and be with her. "Again, I'm sorry, but I can't . . . can't
              help it." One year
and three months ago Rebecca had been diagnosed

              with a rare invasive
cervical cancer. After her hysterectomy and chemo, she had started training
              for a half marathon

again. The surgeon had removed most of Rebecca's lymph nodes,
              thought that she
"had got it all." A week before the race, Rebecca felt unwell. "Probably

              flu," her local
doctor said. "Your immune system has been compromised."
              Both Dave and I

know it's either flu or a recurrence. On YouTube
              I keep watching
Jacqueline du Pré play the Elgar on the *Davydov*,

her Stradivarius cello.
In the silence after she tunes up, the conductor—her new husband,
                    twenty-four-year-old Daniel

Barenboim—raises his eyebrows to ask if she's ready, then nods,
                    gazes over
the orchestra, and lifts his right arm. On the downbeat of his baton

            she bows
those first low virulent notes. Her bow comes crashing down,
                    sawing through pain

like the thick trunk of an oak that lightning has struck and toppled.
                    Fallen, it must
now be cut up and carted away. In 1918, after regaining

            consciousness
from general anesthesia for a tonsillectomy, Elgar had asked
                    for paper and pen,

had written down the melody. Dave once showed me the screensaver
                    on his computer—
a photo of Rebecca and him on their mountain bikes next to a felled

            redwood as wide as they stood tall.
Red-brown hair, blue eyes, she wore a green jersey. She smiled at Dave
                    as a friend snapped

their picture. Du Pré flashes her nervy I-can't-believe-
                    I-just-played-it
smile at Barenboim after she's run through that headlong

hundred-yard dash
of a scherzo, sixteenth-note riffs, at the end of the second movement's
Allegro molto.

It's the intimate smile of a woman playing the instrument
she loves
so that its soundboard vibrates with all her youth and exuberant

being. Just so
Dave and Rebecca smiled at each other from the screensaver.
I can't begin

to imagine the sorrow Dave lives with, though I've known him
twelve years
and he's more older brother to me than therapist.

Maybe
his sadness unsaid is like a huge ungainly cello
that he must lug

in its blue, oversize, plastic case wherever he travels.
He must fly 80,000
miles per year, buy an extra ticket so it can sit

on the seat beside
him. He straps it in with the seat belt. He takes it out
of the plastic case,

practices with it, then plays it for total strangers, who applaud
how human
wooden sorrow sounds. It is an old sorrow. It is the *Davydov*.

                         It was made
in 1712 by Stradivari—alpine spruce seasoned twenty-five years
                  for its belly;

for its back, neck, and ribs deeply flamed native maple
                  to give it
a bell's bronze resonance. He hollowed out back and belly

                  with a large gouge.
Finished them with thumb planes. Cut the f-holes with flutings
                  in the lower wings.

Fitted, trimmed the bass bar. Glued it to the belly, which he then
                  glued to the ribs. Sound post
wedged tight. Scrolled neck outlined on a block, sawn out. Pegbox

                  and volutes carved. Cut
the purfling channel. Black inlay. After the ground coat of varnish dried,
                  he applied the final

reddish oil varnish. All so that this wood might speak, might lament
                  and grow angry
in a voice that cannot be forgotten. Sorrow's instrument

                  got passed down
from one generation of grief to the next. It was given
                  in 1870

to Karl Davydov, whom Tchaikovsky called "the czar
                  of cellists,"
by his patron. It was bought in 1964 for $90,000

---

by Ismena Holland who gave it
to her goddaughter, Jacqueline du Pré. Jacqueline played it for nine years
                    until multiple sclerosis

froze the feeling in her fingertips. She was twenty-eight.
                    Upon her death
at forty-two, it was sold and loaned indefinitely to Yo-Yo Ma. He didn't

                    like the way
she played it, thought that "Jacqueline's unbridled dark qualities
                    went against

the *Davydov*. You have to coax the instrument. The more
                    you attack it,
the less it returns." Dave, Davydov, coax sorrow out

                    of a wooden box strung
with steel, synthetic, or goat-gut strings. Do not attack it. It will return
                    and return to you

your life in complex harmonics heard and unheard. Do not
                    forget it,
as Yo-Yo Ma did his other Stradivarius, the *Montagnana*

                    cello, in a Manhattan
taxicab. Three hours later, the taxi driver Dishashi Lukumwena
                    opened his trunk

and found the cello. Sorrow will be returned to you, to all
                    of us, intact.
Dave, today in my therapy session, you told me, "Whether

                    Rebecca lives or dies,
I want all the more to be alive." *O sing unto the LORD a new song.*
                    Jacqueline du Pré

did not foresee her early death from MS or how for the last decade
                    and a half she wouldn't
play. *Sing unto the LORD with the harp; with the harp, and the voice*

                    of a psalm. In 1967, after
the Six-Day War, she and Daniel got married in Jerusalem. *Let the floods*
                    clap their hands: let the hills

be joyful together. In a railway car, long blonde hair swaying
                    to the train's motion,
TV documentary camera rolling, trees and buildings

                    passing the half-open
window, Jacqueline plays the *Davydov*, no bow. *Let the sea roar,*
                    and the fulness thereof;

the world, and they that dwell therein. She plucks its strings
                    pizzicato, smiles
allegro con fuoco. Wildly she sings a song of her own invention—*Bar*

                    baba bum . . . New wedding ring
glints gold on her finger flying over the fretless black neck. What noise
                    joy makes, keeps making!

Notes

The images described in "Offering Red" are drawn from the exhibition *Hard Rain: The Late Works of Mary Hambleton*, displayed at the Stewart Center Gallery, Purdue University, West Lafayette, Indiana from October 26th through December 6th, 2009. The italicized quotations are taken from "In Conversation: Mary Hambleton with Ron Janowich," *The Brooklyn Rail* (March, 2004), excerpts from which were reprinted in the exhibition's catalogue.

In "Christ's Entry into Brussels in 1889," James Ensor's original canvas depicted many slogans on banners and placards, some of which he later painted over. However, his 1898 etching modeled on the painting preserves the erased slogans, which the poem quotes.

Free Verse Editions

Edited by Jon Thompson

About the Author

Donald Platt is the author of six volumes of poetry. In addition to *Man Praying*, these books include *Tornadoesque, Dirt Angels, My Father Says Grace, Cloud Atlas*, and *Fresh Peaches, Fireworks, & Guns*. His poems have appeared in *The New Republic, American Poetry Review, Poetry, Paris Review, Kenyon Review, Georgia Review, Southwest Review, Ploughshares, Southern Review, Iowa Review*, and *Yale Review*, as well as many other national journals. He is a recipient of two fellowships from the National Endowment for the Arts and three Pushcart Prizes. Three of his poems have been anthologized in *The Best American Poetry* series. He teaches in the MFA program at Purdue University.

Photograph of the author by
Katherine Roeser. Used by permission.

CPSIA information can be obtained
at www.ICGtesting.com
Printed in the USA
LVHW01s2256040318
568649LV00005B/10/P